ideals®
MOTHER'S DAY
Vol. 46, No. 3

Publisher, Patricia A. Pingry
Executive Editor, Cynthia Wyatt
Art Director, Patrick McRae
Production Manager, Jeff Wyatt
Editorial Assistant, Kathleen Gilbert
Copy Editors, Marian Hollyday
Rhonda Colburn

ISBN 0-8249-1073-7

IDEALS—Vol. 46, No. 3 May 1989 IDEALS (ISSN 0019-137X) is published eight times a year: February, March, May, June, August, September, November, December by IDEALS PUBLISHING CORPORATION, Nelson Place at Elm Hill Pike, Nashville, Tenn. 37214. Second class postage paid at Nashville, Tennessee, and additional mailing offices. Copyright © 1989 by IDEALS PUBLISHING CORPORATION. POSTMASTER: Send address changes to Ideals, Post Office Box 148000, Nashville, Tenn. 37214-8000. All rights reserved. Title IDEALS registered U.S. Patent Office.

SINGLE ISSUE—$3.95
ONE-YEAR SUBSCRIPTION—eight consecutive issues as published—$17.95
TWO-YEAR SUBSCRIPTION—sixteen consecutive issues as published—$31.95
Outside U.S.A., add $6.00 per subscription year for postage and handling.

ACKNOWLEDGMENTS

ARE ALL THE CHILDREN IN? by Author Unknown from *THE SPEAKER'S TREASURY OF 400 QUOTABLE POEMS,* Croft M. Pentz, compiler, 1963 by Zondervan Publishing House. Used by permission; DUCK'S DITTY from *THE WIND IN THE WILLOWS* by Kenneth Grahame, Copyright 1908, 1933 by Charles Scribner's Sons; THE SPIRIT OF THE HOME by Edgar A. Guest from *THE PASSING THRONG,* Copyright 1923 by The Reilly & Lee Co. Used by permission; RUNNING WATER by Arthur Guiterman from *DEATH AND GENERAL PUTNAM,* Copyright 1935. All rights reserved; excerpts by H.G. Wells were used by permission of A.P. Watt, Ltd., Literary Agents, London, England. Our sincere thanks to the following whose addresses we were unable to locate: Helen Fitzgerald for MAY; Mabel C. Fuller for MY NEIGHBOR'S WISTERIA from *DAVIS ANTHOLOGY OF NEWSPAPER VERSE 1931* by Franklyn Pierre Davis; Patra Giroux for MOTHERHOOD; Starrlette L. Howard for MOTHER'S WAGES; Sudha Khristmukti for A LITTLE BOY'S LOVES; Bill Nunn for QUIET PLACES; Mary E. Rathfon for GERANIUMS; Fred Toothaker for WHEN I GROW UP from *FIVE TIMES TWENTY;* Mary Pollard Tynes for LOVE COMPANIONS ME from *THE SUNSET HILL,* copyright 1935; B.Y. Williams for MY MOTHER WILL WALK IN HER GARDEN from *FAR IS THE HILL.*

Front and back covers by Robert Cushman Hayes

Inside front cover by Gay Bumgarner

Inside back cover by Ina Mackey

In Blossom-Time

Thomas Curtis Clark

In blossom-time can any say
That life is desolate and gray?
When cherry boughs are drifted snow,
When springtime couriers, singing, go
Through orchard lanes, which for a day
Are very heaven, who could lay
Upon the gods of faraway
One word of blame for fret or woe—
    In blossom-time?

What man could hate or envy know
When apple blossoms burst and blow?
When, free at last, the kindly May
Endeavors Winter's debts to pay—
    In blossom-time?

From *HOME ROADS AND FAR HORIZONS* by Thomas Curtis Clark. Copyright 1935 by Harper & Row, Publishers, Inc. Reprinted by permission of Harper & Row, Publishers, Inc.

Photo Opposite
MEADOW FLOWERS WITH STREAM
H. Armstrong Roberts, Inc.

May

Helen Fitzgerald

May's green apron is decked with flowers
Of every sort and hue:
Marsh marigolds, hepaticas,
Iris bearded and blue.

Lady's-slippers of palest yellow
Bloom in deep woodland dells;
Flowering along dusty roadsides
Are clusters of bluebells.

Violets yellow and purple
Waft fragrance to the breeze;
Trilliums red and white whisper
"Oh, do not pluck us please."

Beautiful bloodroots are flaunting
Their petals white as pearl;
Jack peeps from his little pulpit
To watch fern fronds unfurl.

Photo Opposite
WOODLAND RETREAT
ELLISON BAY, WISCONSIN
Ken Dequaine

My Neighbor's Wisteria

Mabel C. Fuller

My neighbor's wisteria sways in the breeze,
A fair, castled lady of languorous ease,
High in her bower of flowering grace.
One turns to look for her winsome face
In silver-mauve blossoms, wearing a veil
Of ethereal beauty, tender and frail.

Through the long winter months in hiding she lay,
Storing perfume for this warm, sunny day;
Her bower bereft, storm-tossed, and wind-swept,
Drenched by cold clouds that over her wept,
Awaiting in quiet the time to rejoice,
When the birds and all nature pure happiness voice.

Her silken plumes swaying once more in the breeze—
God fashioned her beauty for mortals' heartsease.

Photo Opposite
WISTERIA
Ina Mackey

CRAFTWORKS

Pressed Flower Notes

These lovely cards are made with dried, pressed flowers which are mounted on wax paper and covered with a single layer of facial tissue. A plain white paper liner accommodates greetings and messages.

Materials Needed:
Dried, pressed flowers, leaves, and grasses
Wax paper
White paper
White glue
1 soft bristle brush, 1-1¼ inches wide
Facial tissues, white or pastel
Pinking shears
Iron
Cotton cloth for ironing

Step One: Preparing Backing

Fold and/or cut a piece of white paper to the size that you wish your card to be. Bear in mind the size of the envelope that you will be using. For best results, note cards should not exceed the size of the facial tissues you work with. Cut wax paper to a size slightly larger than the white paper liner.

Step Two: Mounting Flowers

Mix one part white glue with two parts water and brush this solution over the entire wax paper surface using a soft bristle brush. Using the opened paper liner underneath the wax paper as a guide, place dried flowers, leaves, or grasses on the right side of the wax paper. This will be the front of your card.

Note: Tweezers facilitate handling of the delicate petals and grasses.

Separate the layers of tissue by blowing softly at the edge. Place a single thickness of white or pastel tissue over the dried flowers and entire wet surface. Saturate the tissue with the glue solution, stroking gently from the center with the brush to eliminate air bubbles.

Step Three: Assembling Card

After the surface has dried overnight, iron the card between layers of cotton cloth, using the wool setting. Remove the card from the cloth and trim with pinking shears or the serrated edge of the wax paper dispenser. Fold in half to coordinate with paper liner.

Insert the liner into the folded floral panel and secure with a bit of glue at the crease, if desired. Your note cards are ready for use.

Variation: Mrs. Kelley also makes sun-catchers by the same process. She presses the completed wax paper panel into an embroidery hoop, trims away excess, and finishes with a ruffled lace border. These sun-catchers are delightful sights in sunny windows.

Mrs. Alice B. Kelley uses materials from her farm in Connellsville, Pennsylvania, to make these cards and sun-catchers. She sells them in specialty shops at home and tells us that she is delighted to share her crafts with Ideals readers because of the happiness they have brought to others over the years.

Photo Opposite
Gerald Koser

In a Country Garden

Violet Hall

Golden chain, sweet golden chain
That greets us every year,
Dripping down from overhead
When warmer days are near,
Laburnum is too harsh a name
To welcome such as you,
Descanting wealth of sunny days,
Dispelling early dew.

You columbines amongst the grass,
Aquilegia will not fit
Your frail exquisite daintiness
One tiny, little bit;
And what of love-lies-bleeding?
Could any other name
Be as romantic-sounding,
Or ring out quite the same?

Tall, glowing red-hot pokers
In country gardens fair,
Love-in-a-mist, snapdragons,
And bee-kissed others there—
How delightful and well-chosen
Your names must surely be;
But who found them in the first place,
Ah—that's the mystery.

Photo Overleaf
ROSE GARDEN
WINONA, MINNESOTA
Ken Dequaine

Photo Opposite
FLORAL BOUQUET
Comstock

10

My Mother Will Walk in Her Garden

B.Y. Williams

My mother will walk in her garden
  When spring comes over the hill;
She will find the most venturesome snowdrop
  And the earliest daffodil.

She will prune the too-wayward lilac,
  Lift the rose that the wind has tossed—
My mother is very careful
  Lest some small growing thing be lost!

Her marigold seed will be planted,
  Awaiting the soft, warm rain;
Petunias and phlox and zinnias
  Will bloom in bright rows again;

Forgotten will be the long winter
  And conquered the stubborn clod—
My mother keeps faith with springtime;
  My mother keeps faith with God.

14

Mother's Day Delights

Strawberry Topped Meringue Torte

6 egg whites
½ teaspoon cream of tartar
¼ teaspoon salt
1¾ cups sugar
½ teaspoon almond *or* vanilla extract
2 3-ounce packages cream cheese, softened
1 cup sugar
½ teaspoon almond extract *or* 1 teaspoon vanilla extract
2 cups heavy cream, whipped
2 cups miniature multicolored marshmallows
2 to 3 packages frozen strawberries, thawed

In a large bowl beat egg whites, cream of tartar, and salt until foamy. Gradually beat in 1¾ cups sugar (1 tablespoon at a time). Using high speed of mixer, beat until stiff and glossy. Add ½ teaspoon extract; mix well. Spread in a buttered 9 × 13-inch pan. Bake in a 275° oven for 60 minutes. Turn off oven and let cake set in oven at least 12 hours. *Do not open oven door.* Blend cream cheese, remaining sugar, and extract until fluffy. Carefully fold in whipped cream and marshmallows; spread over meringue. Chill 24 hours. Top with strawberries. Serves 12.

Strawberry Torte Fluff

½ cup flour
¼ cup brown sugar
¼ cup margarine
⅓ cup chopped pecans
2 tablespoons lemon juice
1 7-ounce jar marshmallow creme
1 16-ounce package frozen strawberries, thawed
2 cups heavy cream, whipped

Combine flour and sugar; cut in margarine. Add nuts. Press into the bottom of a 9-inch springform pan. Bake in a 350° oven 20 minutes. Cool. Slowly add lemon juice to marshmallow creme. Mix until well blended. Stir in strawberries; fold in whipped cream. Pour over crumb crust. Freeze until serving time. Serves 8 to 10.

Coconut Strawberry Torte

1 10-ounce package frozen strawberries
2 envelopes unflavored gelatin
¾ cup sugar
¼ teaspoon salt
2 eggs, separated
3 8-ounce packages cream cheese, room temperature
Red food coloring
1 cup heavy cream, whipped
1 cup flaked coconut
Fresh strawberries, sliced

Drain syrup from strawberries and set aside. In top of double boiler combine gelatin, ¾ cup sugar, and salt. Beat together strawberry syrup and egg yolks and add to gelatin mixture. Heat over simmering water 10 minutes. Cool to room temperature and add thawed strawberries; stir. Whip cheese until fluffy. Beat in strawberry mixture and food coloring. Chill. Stir occasionally until mixture mounds when dropped from a spoon. Beat egg whites until stiff but not dry. Fold into gelatin. Fold in whipped cream. Pour into a 9-inch round springform pan. Sprinkle with half of the coconut. Chill several hours. When ready to serve, run knife dipped in hot water around the edge of pan and remove torte. Press remaining coconut into sides and top of cake. Garnish with sliced strawberries. Serves 14.

Strawberry Pineapple Salad

1 8-ounce package cream cheese, softened
3 tablespoons honey
2 cups strawberries, hulled and crushed
1 cup crushed pineapple, drained

Combine cream cheese and honey in a bowl. Add strawberries and pineapple; blend well. Pour into a freezer tray and freeze 2 hours. Cut into 4 portions. Serve on lettuce leaves and garnish with strawberry slices, if desired. Serves 4.

Photo opposite
Strawberry Pineapple Salad

— Cynthia Wyatt —

1939 World's Fair poster by John Atherton
The Trylon and Perisphere, seen on this poster, symbolize the "World of the Future."

Fifty years ago the New York World's Fair opened its doors to the public. Over the next two years, forty-five million of us paid our seventy-five cent admission and entered the future—the "World of Tomorrow" they called it.

We walked over sixty-five miles of pathways; we saw the new arts, the new car designs, the new kitchens, the new factories, and the new highways which would eventually revolutionize our lives. We saw the first television broadcasts: David Sarnoff, president of RCA, and President Roosevelt giving speeches in Washington, D.C., while we watched in New York.

We made our way to the center of the Fair, the Trylon and Perisphere which epitomized in architecture our immanent thrust out of "the dark ages" of the present into a towering, gleaming tomorrow. We entered the 700-foot tall Trylon, crossed a sixty-five-foot high bridge into the 200-foot diameter Perisphere, and beheld, as we circled its great bowl, a diorama of "Democracity," a dream of industry, culture, and housing where a theoretical population of one and a half million could live and work.

A city called "Centerton" was the cultural hub where 250,000 employees worked, researched, taught, performed, created, and were entertained. Most of this population commuted, thanks to sleek modern transportation, to what we now think of as suburbs—"Pleasantvilles" with populations of 10,000 and "Millvilles" with populations of 25,000 which dotted the countryside surrounding Centerton. Broad highways wove together the homes, work places, factories, recreational parks, and historic preserves. We saw no pollution, no poverty, no unemployment, no slums. Instead, we saw the best which planning can accomplish.

We were promised that by 1962 we would turn our menial labors over to sophisticated machinery and spend our spare time in pursuit of culture and art. Far from robbing men of their jobs, machines would increase human productivity to such a pitch that everybody would be busy.

We wandered through the exhibit halls of General Motors, General Electric, Chrysler, RCA, Ford, and Westinghouse Electric, marveling at the electric dishwashers, electric stoves, and GE's fanciful light displays in the "House of Magic." General Motors put us in easy chairs and carried us along a fifteen-minute tour of car designs as beautiful as jewelry. U.S. Steel invited us to witness the workings of a great ore mine and the gigantic furnaces which produce the metal for steel.

Music revues were everywhere, and police even closed down a cabaret somewhere on the fairgrounds where the dancers were too scantily clad. We chose from hundreds of food vendors, all too expensive.

Photographs courtesy of The Queens Museum, New York

One of them told us the prices were high because they had to pay a stiff tariff out of their profits to the Fair officials.

Ironically, the seventy-five cent admission for adults was hard on the average family. We were at the end of a decade of Depression economics and were still worried about jobs, housing, and education for our children. The Fair, which cost $157,000,000, did not turn a profit.

Westinghouse's robots making the housewife's world an easy one, General Electric's "talking" kitchens, the sign of things to come in Pontiac's transparent plastic car bodies, and the "democratic" uniformity of mass-produced goods were on their way to us whether we could pay the cost of admission or not. The real question posed by the 1939 World's Fair was, What would the people who lived in "Democracity" in 1962 be like?

H.G. Wells, the visionary writer of science fiction, instructed us to take to heart the future which the World's Fair revealed. He stated in an article published by The *New York Times* in 1939, "The World's Fair in New York is to differ from most World's Fairs in being a forward-looking display. Its keynotes are not history and glory but practical anticipation and hope. It is to present the World of Tomorrow. . . .

"So the visitor who wants to get the most out of this World's Fair will do best to regard it not as a show of things but as. . . a gathering of live objects, each of which is going to do something to him, possibly something quite startling, before he is very much older. . . .

"It is so close a Tomorrow that it is almost Today when it will be possible for a dozen or a score of men to sit in conference, seeing and hearing each other by radio, television, telephone, when bodily they are hundreds of miles apart. . . .

"When I was young I used to think of old people going home to some 'Haven of Rest.' I doubt that now. I find myself at seventy-two with far more wanderlust than I had forty years ago, and I perceive that most of my elder contemporaries wind up their careers with a tour round the globe. So long as it is reasonably comfortable, the old are as eager for travel as any one."

On behalf of all of us, Westinghouse Electric Corporation buried a time capsule to be opened five thousand years in the future in the year 6939. The capsule contained articles of clothing, seeds, money, maps, textile samples, and commonly used health, cosmetic, and safety products, as well as such treasures as a Mickey Mouse child's cup; reproductions of paintings by Picasso, Mondrian, and Dali; a copy of both the novel and the smash hit movie, "Gone With the Wind"; several newspapers, including the *Daily Worker*; the Sears, Roebuck catalogue; and footage, poignant in light of Germany's refusal to participate in the Fair, of Jesse Owens winning the 100-meter dash for America at the 1936 Berlin Olympics.

The World's Fair was built, like much of human aspiration, on 1,216 acres of useless swampland. The fiftieth anniversary of the World's Fair raises questions about the ability of technology alone to make the World of Tomorrow all it should be. As H.G. Wells advised us, our burden is to use technology to transform the world into a brotherhood of knowledge, optimism, and hope.

The Queens Museum in Flushing, New York, houses a large collection of World's Fair memorabilia—everything from guidebooks and souvenir pins to such novelty items as the NYWF radio, seen below.

Souvenir radio from the 1939 World's Fair   Photograph by Phyllis Bilick

HAPPY MOTHER'S DAY

Irene Larsen

I wish you joy and laughter,
No doubts or times of fear,
Love forever after
Through all of your many years.

I wish you sunshine and roses,
Blue skies for every day,
And, as each day closes,
Starlight to grace the way.

I wish you friendship's warming hand
And doors that never close,
Rolling tides and silver sands,
God's blessings—all of those.

I wish you moonlight and rainbows,
A prayer to wrap around your day,
All the good things, heaven knows,
And a super Mother's Day.

A Slice of Life

Edgar A. Guest

Dishes to wash and clothes to mend,
　　And always another meal to plan,
Never the tasks of a mother end
　　And oh, so early her day began!
Floors to sweep and the pies to bake,
And chairs to dust and the beds to make.

Oh, the home is fair when you come at night
　　And the meal is good and the children gay,
And the kettle sings in its glad delight
　　ʹAnd the mother smiles in her gentle way;
So great her love that you seldom see
Or catch a hint of the drudgery.

Home, you say, when the day is done,
　　Home to comfort and peace and rest;
Home, where the children romp and run—
　　There is the place that you love the best!
Yet what would the home be like if you
Had all of its endless tasks to do?

Would it be home if she were not there,
　　Brave and gentle and fond and true?
Could you so fragrant a meal prepare?
　　Could you the numberless duties do?
What were the home that you love so much,
Lacking her presence and gracious touch?

She is the spirit of all that's fair;
　　She is the home that you think you build;
She is the beauty you dream of there;
　　She is the laughter with which it's filled—
She, with her love and her gentle smile,
Is all that maketh the home worthwhile.

Edgar A. Guest began his illustrious career in 1895 at the age of fourteen when his work appeared in the Detroit Free Press. *His column was syndicated in over 300 newspapers, and he became known as "The Poet of the People." Mr. Guest captured the hearts of vast radio audiences with his weekly program, "It Can Be Done" and, until his death in 1959, published many treasured volumes of poetry.*

Walk Gently

Lou Rogers Wehlitz

Walk gently down this garden path.
Each flower blooms this very hour
To give to you some secret power.
Each blossom's own sweet whispered word
In silence only can be heard.

Be quiet—very quiet as you pass
And you will see a tiny blade of grass
Bend softly to the wily wind,
Nodding back as friend to friend.
The shadowy trees are standing guard,
Their leaves rustling in one accord.

The butterfly is poised in grace
Above the flower's lovely face.
The striped bee, who, buzzing close to you,
Is searching budding cups of honeydew.
Each bird comes here to sing a song
Where faith and peace and joy belong.

Walk gently down this garden path.
You will hear secrets as you pass,
Find peace and joy within your grasp.
There's comfort here for you to take;
Walk gently for your own dear sake.

Photo Opposite
BLOSSOMING GARDEN PATH
WILMINGTON, DELAWARE
Gottlieb Hampfler

Angels in Disguise

Reginald Holmes

There is a sweet, angelic look
In every mother's eyes
That makes us stop and wonder
If they're angels in disguise;

For they are always standing by
When someone needs a friend.
No one has as much compassion;
None are quicker to defend.

There is a little bit of God
In every mother's heart.
He molded them of finer clay
That sets them well apart.
They are an earthly blessing
That heaven itself supplies;
And so we can't help believing
They are angels in disguise!

Mother's Hands

Lois J. Funk

Mother's hands were busy hands,
But never did they fail
To take the time to tie a bow
Or braid a loose pigtail.
And never did those hands refuse
To soothe a fevered brow,
So even injured dolls pulled through
In Mother's hands, somehow.

It seemed those hands were magic,
Always knowing where to start
To reconstruct a shattered dream
Or mend a broken heart.

Dear Lord, I pray, as years go by,
Whatever life's demands,
That I may give just half the love
I've found in Mother's hands.

My Cinderella Grandmother

Kathleen M. Gilbert

If opportunity and circumstances had not been obstacles in my grandmother's life, she would have become a famous fashion designer. She would have purchased exquisite fabrics to dress the world's most beautiful women, choreographed extravagant fashion shows, attended lavish banquets, and lived a Cinderella life of gold, glass, and glitter. Instead, Grandmother was to spend her life venting her creativity on her daughter and granddaughter.

Grandmother became familiar with the clothing industry while she was employed as a seamstress in New York City's garment district. It was there that she would tediously cut and sew pieces of material together all day long for most of her life. With no opportunity for self-expression, she performed the repetitive tasks like an assembly-line robot of the early twentieth century. It was in these minutes and hours that she would mentally design our stylish clothing.

Mother and I spent countless hours with Grandmother as she tailored her patterns to our unique and somewhat challenging figures. Mother stood only five feet tall, and I, going through the awkward stages of adolescence, was taller but carried a waistless torso upon toothpick-like legs. What made matters worse was the irregular full-length mirror we used to view ourselves. It never failed to accentuate our less desirable features!

Grandmother was so fluid in her movements as she pinned us from collar to hem. She was like a whirlwind, moving from her knees to a standing position while tucking fabric under her chin or arms and pulling out lengths to be measured. And as she stuffed her lips with the heads of pins, she would mumble, "Kathleen, never put pins in your mouth. You could swallow them!"

Our times together became a tradition as we shared plenty of good food, good conversation, and good laughs. There was usually a pot of Grandmother's tomato sauce filled with meatballs and sausage simmering on the stove and other delicacies like baked, garlic-stuffed mushrooms and artichokes just waiting to be eaten. We'd laugh at ourselves over the silliest things—especially as we grew more tired, for Grandmother worked relentlessly for hours on end. Getting stuck with pins wasn't one of my favorite things, but it was inevitable and guaranteed a round of laughter. And there were those moments when, in the course of some conversations, my young mind was not privy to pertinent information. To remedy that situation, Mother and Grandmother would substitute Italian for English wherever necessary. And no matter how hard I insisted, they refused to let me in on their little secrets or teach me to speak their Sicilian dialect!

But Grandmother would never lose her concentration as she went from us to the sewing machine, then to the ironing board and back to us again, all the while in conversation. She had to finish what she began. Even though Mother's and my stamina would begin to wane in the late hours of the evening, there would usually be one last touch that needed to be added. And when the garment was completed to Grandmother's satisfaction, she would stand back and have us turn around and around. Then she would compliment us on how beautiful we looked in our new clothing! There were times, however, when her passion for the art kept her up and sewing long after we'd gone home. Her creativity was free to soar within the confines of her home during those peaceful early hours of the morning.

Grandmother must have found much more contentment in dressing us than she ever could have dressing temperamental models. Perhaps her life was like Cinderella's after all, in that she found enjoyment and fulfillment in being with and doing for her loved ones.

Photo Opposite
SCISSORS AND PINS
Fred Sieb

Country CHRONICLE

—Lansing Christman—

In the 1920s I was a boy growing up in the country, and my high school was ten miles away from home. For the four years I attended the school, I rode the train both ways, five times a week, just as my older brothers and sisters had done before me.

Each morning and afternoon the train passed a weathered farmhouse, and each day there stood on the back lawn a gingham-aproned woman waving a small, white handkerchief. I always waved back. That woman was my mother.

She observed this ritual for eighteen years until all of her nine children finished high school. I was the youngest and the last to graduate, but she never failed to appear as the train sped by. She was there in winter's snow and in spring's flowering days of apple and lilac blooms. She hailed me in summer's heat waves and in the blaze of autumn's glorious hues.

I deeply cherish my memories of the devoted farm woman who raised me. She worked in the kitchen and garden to provide our nourishment for body and soul alike. She loved birds and flowers, the rolling hills and meadows around us, and the sweeping pastures and distant woodland rills.

At times I can still see my mother, her silver

Country CHRONICLE
———Lansing Christman———

In the 1920s I was a boy growing up in the country, and my high school was ten miles away from home. For the four years I attended the school, I rode the train both ways, five times a week, just as my older brothers and sisters had done before me.

Each morning and afternoon the train passed a weathered farmhouse, and each day there stood on the back lawn a gingham-aproned woman waving a small, white handkerchief. I always waved back. That woman was my mother.

She observed this ritual for eighteen years until all of her nine children finished high school. I was the youngest and the last to graduate, but she never failed to appear as the train sped by. She was there in winter's snow and in spring's flowering days of apple and lilac blooms. She hailed me in summer's heat waves and in the blaze of autumn's glorious hues.

I deeply cherish my memories of the devoted farm woman who raised me. She worked in the kitchen and garden to provide our nourishment for body and soul alike. She loved birds and flowers, the rolling hills and meadows around us, and the sweeping pastures and distant woodland rills.

At times I can still see my mother, her silver

hair shining in the sun or glowing softly in the lamplight as she sewed in the evening. I can see the twinkle in her eyes and the cheerful smile she always seemed to wear.

Mother has long been gone from the homestead, and I live nearly a thousand miles closer to the coast. Even the distance and time itself cannot diminish her gifts to us. Her capacity to love us all, to wave us on as we took our big steps in life lives on in my memory. And on Mother's Day, I'll walk with those memories down a hedge of lilacs in their peak of bloom. I'll stop by the fragrant pinxter bush, the flower that mother so loved, which grows along the garden wall. I'll gently touch the fronds of ferns lining the dooryard walk, and she will be there. I will be comforted and consoled as I was all those years ago when she waved me on to do my best and become the man I am today.

The author of two published books, Lansing Christman has been contributing to Ideals *for almost twenty years. Mr. Christman has also been published in several American, foreign, and braille anthologies. He and his wife, Lucile, live in rural South Carolina where they enjoy the pleasures of the land around them.*

Geraniums

Mary E. Rathfon

My mother loved geraniums,
And I can see them still
In lovely blooms of pink and red
Upon her window sill.

She gave each one such tender care
And watered them just so.
By watching as she fussed with them,
I knew they had to grow.

I also tried geraniums—
Red, pink, white and others.
But mine grew pale and died away.
None ever got like Mother's.

Many years have passed since then,
And only recently,
I stopped before a florist's shop
Where, waiting just for me,

Pots of bright geraniums
Invited me to buy.
I thought again of Mother's blooms
And whispered, ''I will try!''

I planted them along the fence
Beside the other flowers,
Where they were caressed by morning sun
And drenched with summer showers.

Now I view from my window sill
Geraniums like no others.
None ever were more beautiful—
That is, except my mother's.

Photo Opposite
FRENCH DOORS
International Stock Photography

Morning Thankfulness

D. A. Hoover

I hear a bird's first silver note,
Melodious from the lawn—
A beautiful awakening,
Another glorious dawn.

I find my robe and slippers
And tiptoe down the stairs.
The family's gently sleeping;
My heart is filled with prayer.

I'm thankful I can rise and walk
And feel so happy too,
To guide and serve my family
With love this whole day through.

I see the morning star grow pale,
Pink, sun-washed from the sky
And thank the Lord no mother is
More fortunate than I!

34

This Day

Esther Kem Thomas

The nicest things I have enjoyed today—
A pot of garden beans, a slim bouquet
Of brown-eyed susans in an earthen vase,
A friendly call, a spider web of lace

With dewdrop sequins, and a sample jar
Of new-made jelly. First, the morning star
Bequeathed this day to me while at my feet
The puppy rolled and stretched; the day was sweet

With odd variety—a daughter's eyes
To peek with me at browning apple pies;
At noon a shaft of gold lay on my floor,
And children, laughing, clamored at the door;

When evening threw its shadow on the lawn,
Then I was thankful! I had seen the dawn
Lay hold upon a day and mark it mine
And bind it round with shining, sacred twine

Made from the endless charms life can crochet
Into the pleasant routine of a day!

Photo Overleaf
THE LAPHAM-PATTERSON HOUSE
A NATIONAL HISTORIC LANDMARK
THOMASVILLE, GEORGIA
Ken Dequaine

Housewife's Lament

Caryl M. Kerber

Make the beds, bandage heads,
Straighten up the room;
Wash the windows, cut the grass,
See the tulips bloom.

Drive the children to school,
Drive them back again.
Have the Cubs to meeting,
Then I clean the den.

Serve on my committee,
Attend the P.T.A.
Forgot to buy the children shoes. . . .
Can't do it today.

Pay the bills, write a note,
Fill the cookie jar.
Oh dear, I forgot to go
And have them grease the car.

Catch up on the ironing,
Scrub the kitchen floor.
Answer phone and doorbell,
Need I list some more?

My pet peeve I must admit,
You surely will agree,
When someone asks, "Are you employed?"
I answer, "No, not me."

To a Young Mother

Naomi Higgs

These are precious, precious moments,
Let delight shine in your eyes;
Drown your tears in pools of laughter;
They're gone before you realize.

Each day brings a special rainbow
That only you can see;
You have your wealth, your pot of gold;
Carry it exultantly.

These are days of vintage wine
To be slowly sipped and tasted.
Hold your goblet carefully,
Lest one tiny drop be wasted.

Like treasured notes and photographs,
Store these moments safely away,
Tenderly and lovingly,
To be unwrapped another day.

Photo Opposite
FEEDING THE GOLDFISH
H. Armstrong Roberts, Inc.

Cookie Jar Memories

Virginia Blanck Moore

Sometimes, when I'm mixing and baking
To fill a cookie jar,
I smell the sweet and spicy air,
And my thoughts are carried far,

To years to come when they'll be grown—
Our cookie-loving clan—
Each girl become a mother too,
Each boy become a man.

I wonder if they won't recall
Such childhood days as this,
Being greeted after school
With cookies and a kiss.

I am somehow sure they will,
For my own memory
Is full of loving greetings
My mother gave to me.

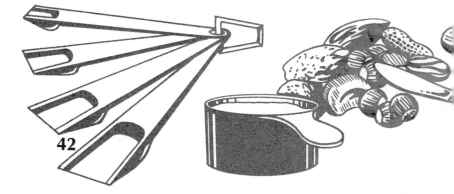

Surprise Cake!

June Masters Bacher

Did I add the cream of tartar;
Beat the egg whites "to a peak"?
What's a "little pinch of soda"?
Oh, I wish a book could speak!

Did I grease the tube pan "lightly"?
Just how long should "one dash" be?
"Do not open up the oven. . . ."
Is it rising? I can't see!

How much is a "double handful"?
Can't a "lump" be any size?
It's small wonder Grandma named it:
"Favorite Cake—A Sure Surprise!"

If I don't look, I'll regret it;
If I do, it's sure to fall;
Either way it's fifty-fifty;
Her "Surprise" will shock us all!

43

Motherhood

I showed my daughter the ducks today;
Enthusiasm she did not lack.
In fact, she almost fell in the pond
When one let out a quack.

You see, my friends, she's only one
And to her all things are new.
Adults take things for granted;
She has her own point of view.

She thinks it is a splendid thing
To catch a raindrop in her hand.
To walk barefoot in the lush, green grass
Is something really grand.

Playing ''get ya'' with her dad
Produces a case of giggles.
At times I'm lucky to get a hug
In between the squirms and wiggles.

Oh, baby girl of mine,
I hope your years are free and good,
And maybe some day, you too
Can experience the rewards of motherhood.

Patra Giroux
Apple Creek, Ohio

A Little Boy's Loves

A little boy's loves
Are as many as the number
Of secrets that he likes to keep;
Tender as the tiny shoot
Of spring's first newborn leaf,
And real as the many fairies
Prancing in his dreams.
He thinks of them first thing each morning
And hugs them tight at night;
Then he digs them out on rainy days
When the sun must hide from open fields.
Or he tells them to his bosom friend
If it might please his will.
You might see that blushing cheek
As now he chases some fluffy cloud,
Or when he offers to his lady love
Wildflowers beneath the amber sky.
Look gentle upon such moments sweet
Should the spell be broken and
Childhood's fancies fly;
To him his loves are fair enough
To simply have to be understood.

Ms. Sudha Khristmukti
Gujarat, India

44

Reflections

Mother's Wages

She is paid in dandelions, crayoned art,
And plaster hand prints.
She is also paid in sounds of small voices
In prayer, song, and laughter.

A mother isn't paid by the hour or mile;
She fills her heart with a kiss and a smile.
She can find wealth in clean little faces,
In hugs and in curls, in denims and laces.
She is paid with the sights of little-sized joys.

A mother isn't paid by the hour or mile;
She fills her heart with a kiss and a smile.

Starrlette L. Howard
Layton, Utah

Editor's Note: Readers are invited to submit unpublished, original poetry, short anecdotes, and humorous reflections on life for possible publication in future *Ideals* issues. Please send copies only; manuscripts will not be returned. Writers receive $10 for each published submission. Send material to "Readers' Reflections," Ideals Publishing Corporation, P.O. Box 140300, Nashville, Tennessee 37214-0300.

Lullaby

I held my child as he lay dreaming
Of secrets that he could not share;
While the moon above was gleaming
I whispered to my babe this prayer:

May you learn to love and give;
Unselfish hearts know how to live.
May you grow up brave and strong,
To fight for truth and change all wrong.
May you know the joy of peace,
The songs of birds, the power of seas.
May you soar in freedom's skies
With creative soul and mind that's wise.
May all others come to say,
'He made the difference who passed this way.'

I gently rocked my sleeping son,
My arms protecting him from fear;
But my heart knew he was the one
Whose course he'd have to steer.

Pamela Debs
Tulsa, Oklahoma

THROUGH MY WINDOW

Pamela Kennedy

I'm not sure if it is written somewhere that mothers must have magic, but I know it's true. I've never met a mother yet who didn't have a certain mystical power. All children know about it. Even some fathers are in on the secret, for I've often heard them exclaim in utter frustration, "Go see your mother about it!" Yes, it cannot be denied. Mothermagic exists.

I guess we first encounter it when we are still tiny tots. No one has to tell us that those unreasonable fears about what is lurking under the bed or waiting to lunge from darkened closets can be banished with just a look from Mother. Somehow her presence causes all evil forces to flee. Only benevolent mysteries surround Mother—like the Sandman and the Tooth Fairy and Santa's helpers. No doubt about it; Mothermagic is mighty strong stuff when it comes to banishing the powers of the dark.

And then there are its healing properties. Everyone knows how a mother's kiss can heal the worst bump on the head or bang on the knee. Or how only Mother can apply the antiseptic and bandage so it won't hurt when you pull it off. And is there ever a cooler hand than Mother's when she strokes a fevered brow? It's Mothermagic, pure and simple.

Somehow mothers always know what's going on too. Ever notice how a mother can tell not only who stole the cookies, but exactly how many the culprit took? Or how mothers always seem to have eyes in the backs of their heads and are able to detect the least disobedience without even looking? And how about the way a mother can look into your eyes and see right through to your brain, detecting the smallest lie or even mere exaggeration! There's no other way to explain it. It must be Mothermagic.

When I was small I didn't really understand about Mothermagic. It was just sort of there, like the sun and the stars and clean sheets every week. But when I was about ten, I began to seriously consider this strange phenomenon. How was it that Mother could make me a costume for the class play or Halloween, even when I forgot to tell her I needed it until that morning before school? How was it she always knew what made me sad or happy, where my lost socks were, and answers to questions like why does it rain? How could one woman be so amazing?

As I entered my teens I began to depend upon Mothermagic more and more. "How do you make your hair go this way, Mom?" "Do you know what I can put in this to make it taste better?" "What can I wear to the dance?" "What will I do if he wants to kiss me?" Mother always had the answer; not just any answer, but the right one.

And then, when I left home, I found I didn't need Mothermagic much anymore. I was really pretty smart myself. Besides, it was always available if I got into any really BIG trouble. That's the great thing about Mothermagic—it's there whether you need it or not!

We talked about it once, my Mother and I, and I asked her where she got all that Mothermagic. She just smiled and looked mysterious and said something about finding out for myself one day. But I really wasn't interested just then. I was too busy being busy.

Then one day I had a baby. He was a lovely little bundle with rosy cheeks and blueberry eyes and dandelion fluff for hair. We spent lots of nights, he and I, rocking by the open window, singing lullabies to the moon, and I began to feel the magic creeping in. It came silently, bit by bit, as I held him and listened to his heart beat against mine. I learned I could make him smile with my eyes and calm his tears with my touch! I knew not only when he wanted to eat, but what; and only I could decipher his baby coos and gurgles.

Suddenly I knew I had found the magic. There would be band-aids and fevers and maybe even broken hearts, but I would be able to handle them. I couldn't wait to tell my mother.

"Guess what?!" I announced to her. "I've got it! I've got Mothermagic!"

She smiled that smile I knew so well as she gave me a hug. Then the old look came over her face and she whispered, "I already knew you had it!"

Pamela Kennedy is a freelance writer of short stories, articles, essays, and children's books. Married to a naval officer and mother of three children, she has made her home on both U.S. coasts and currently resides in Hawaii. She draws her material from her own experiences and memories, adding bits of imagination to create a story or mood.

Are All the Children In?

Author Unknown

I think ofttimes, as the night draws nigh,
Of an old house on the hill,
Of a yard all wide and blossom-starred,
Where the children played at will.
And when the night at last came down,
Hushing the merry din,
Mother would look all around and ask,
"Are all the children in?"

'Tis many and many a year since then,
And the old house on the hill
No longer echoes to childish feet,
And the yard is still, so still.
But I see it all as the shadows creep,
And though many the years have been
Since then, I can hear the mother ask,
"Are all the children in?"

I wonder if, when the shadows fall,
On the last, short earthly day,
When we say good-bye to the world outside,
All tired with our childish play,
When we meet the Lover of boys and girls,
Whose own we have always been,
Will we hear Him ask as Mother did,
"Are all the children in?"

Photo Opposite
HOME PATHWAY
Comstock

Mother's Favorite ABC's

Donna Tabbert Long

A baby's yawn
Birthday cakes with one candle
Children chasing soap bubbles
Dandelions picked just for her
Easter baskets
First graders in yellow rainslickers
Giggles
Holding small hands
Identical twins (someone else's)
Jumpropes
Keepsakes
Little fat toes
Marshmallows in cocoa for breakfast
Naps
Owies kissed and made better
Prayers at bedtime
Quiet time
Remembering
Small bunny slippers
Thank you's
Under the covers
Valentines handmade
Whispered secrets
X-tra hugs in the morning
Yes, Mom
Zippers that work

My Grandmother Taught Me...

Kathy Kahn

That God would provide.
How to laugh at myself.
That it was impolite to wipe my nose on my sleeve.
Patience and endurance.
To always try.
To wash my hands and face before coming to the table
    or going to bed.
How to compromise.
How to listen.
To always check for wood ticks after a walk in the
    June woods.
How to remove them.
The joy of reading and listening to stories.
To not give up.
To replenish what you take.
That green apples are better with salt.
To never throw anything away.
How to plant a garden.
To love myself.
To see the best in others.
Where to find the biggest berries.
How to keep the mosquitoes away so you could
    pick them.
That laps *ARE* made for someone you love.
That arms are for someone to hold
And hands are for folding in prayer.

From A *Child's Garden of Verses* by Robert Louis Stevenson, illustrated by Laura Lydecker
Published by Ideals Publishing Corp., Nashville, TN 37214

Looking-Glass River

Robert Louis Stevenson

Smooth it glides upon its travel,
  Here a wimple, there a gleam—
    Oh, the clean gravel!
    Oh, the smooth stream!

Sailing blossoms, silver fishes,
  Paven pools as clear as air—
    How a child wishes
    To live down there!

We can see our colored faces
  Floating on the shaken pool
    Down in cool places
    Dim and very cool;

Till a wind or water wrinkle,
  Dipping martin, plumping trout,
    Spreads in a twinkle
    And blots all out.

See the rings pursue each other;
  All below grows black as night,
    Just as if Mother
    Had blown out the light!

Patience, children, just a minute—
  See the spreading circles die;
    The stream and all in it
    Will clear by-and-by.

When I Grow Up

Fred Toothaker

My mom, she knows my appetite
Cannot be trusted far;
So when she's finished bakin', she
Conceals the cookie jar.

She says that I'm a glutton just
Exactly like my pop;
An' when I start to eatin' sweets,
I don't know where to stop.

I wonder why it is that boys
Can't eat the things they please,
Instead of spinach, carrots, an'
A lot of cottage cheese.

If kids were not supposed to have
The food they like so well,
Just why do mothers cook the things
That are so good to smell?

When I have finished growin' up,
I bet I'll eat the stuff
That I have always wanted but
Of which I never had enough.

Growing Up

Faye A. Eckel

"I love you, Mommy," says a boy
When he is only three;
At eight he thinks he's much too big
To climb upon your knee.

But when he's scrubbed and ready for bed
And saying his tenth good night,
He'll snuggle close and say, "Hey, Mom,
I love you lots tonight."

When he's sixteen and starts to date
And needs the family car,
He'll yell, "It's clean! I love you, Ma!
I won't go fast or far."

At seventeen he's out of school
And soon is miles away.
The scribbled notes he sends to you
End, "Love you much today."

He's grown up to be quite a man;
Handsome, strong, and tall;
But when he's hurt or blue or sad,
He still seems very small.

He's called me Mommy, Mom, and Ma,
And once a year it's Mother.
Soon there will be another name;
He'll call and say, "Grandmother!"

To Mama with Love

Clara Belle Ream

Some say it's just a buttercup
And hurry right on by,
But this quiet, fragile beauty
Caught a very small child's eye.

A chubby hand then plucked it
For Mama, his first bouquet.
She pressed it close against her heart
And wiped a tear away.

We Left You at the Door

James Singleton

We took you down to school today,
  You're just beginning now;
      Although this year you're six years old,
        You seem so young, somehow!
We didn't take you all the way,
  For we'd been told before,
      "Don't go into his room with him.
        Just leave him at the door."

Up to this time we've always gone
  Together everywhere,
      And we have had a lot of fun
        While traveling here and there;
But I well knew before it came,
  We're parted more and more;
      So many times we'll stand outside
        And leave you at the door.

You're growing up so very fast,
   It's hard to keep in step;
      The fact of changing years is hard
         For parents to accept.
You'll have to walk your path alone
   No matter what's in store;
      We'll bring you up to life's classroom,
         Then leave you at the door.

While you were ours these tender years,
   We treasured every day,
      Full knowing that the time would come,
         When you would go your way;
And though this love will still remain,
   Within the heart's deep core,
      Our eyes will sting to see you go—
         And leave us at the door!

Photo Overleaf
CASCADES GARDEN, BANFF
ALBERTA, CANADA
Gene Ahrens

Fulfillment

Nelle Hardgrove

I'm spending today
    with my little ones,
Ignoring the work to be done.
Tomorrow I'll dust
    and sweep the rooms
But right now I'm having fun!

We'll play some games
    and read some books
And I'll hold them close to me!
I won't even think
    of cooking today
For their tea table's set for three!

And later on
    when the shadows fall
And nighttime prayers are said,
I'll tuck them in
    with all my love
And sit there by their bed!

Oh, what a wonderful day
    it will be
Just my little ones and me!
I'll recapture the past
    with my photographs
And savor each memory.

I Like Housecleaning

Dorothy Brown Thompson

It's fun to clean house.
   The food isn't much,
And paint's all about
   That we mustn't touch;
But strange store-away things,
Not like everyday things,
Make marvelous playthings
   From attics and such.

The boxes come out
   From closets and chests,
With odd sorts of clothes
   Like old hats and vests,
And photographed faces,
And ribbons and laces,
And postcards of places,
   And cards left by guests.

Then Mother says, "Throw
   The whole lot away!"
And Father says, "Wait—
   I'll need this someday."
But either way's meaning
A chance to go gleaning
Among the housecleaning
   For new things to play!

Running Water

Arthur Guiterman

By running water let me rest,
By some rebellious fountain
That cleaves a crag where eagles nest
And tumbles down a mountain,
That leaves a canyon's rugged walls
For pleasant woods, and doubles
Around a ridge in laughing falls,
All rainbow-spray and bubbles.

Soft mosses clothe the living rock
Where running water gushes;
To running water bluebirds flock
With tanagers and thrushes—
As visions flock where lightly flows
The mountain's wayward daughter,
For poems are revealed to those
Who rest by running water.

Photo Opposite
HECTOR FALLS
HECTOR, NEW YORK
Dietrich Photography

Quiet Places

Bill Nunn

Quiet.

It's a nice word. A comfortable word. It doesn't intrude. It requires nothing of its viewer. It is peaceful in its lack of complexity. It is soothing to contemplate.

The word's connotations are many and varied. It can evoke many images—the satisfied stillness of a warm home late at night after the children are asleep upstairs in bed; the pleasant lack of action, lying flat-backed in a summery meadow, watching scudding clouds in high skies; or the feeling of time, hushed, standing still in a place of natural beauty.

But the word denotes something that is fairly uniform and widely accepted—a quiescence, intangible and ethereal, but answering a basic, visceral, and spiritual yearning in man.

Quiet is a paradox. It implies an auditory vacuum, but all of its definitions—stillness, silence, tranquility—describe an absence of sound. What is more welcome than the hush that follows a sudden cessation of cacophonous assaults on battered eardrums? Or what is more pervasive than the ominous "quiet before the storm"?

While this does not necessarily mean that there are different kinds of quiet, it does imply variations in the awareness and appreciation of quiet, simply because of the nature of the sounds that precede it or follow it.

But where is quiet? How can it be found? It resides in nature's secluded places, in the welling up of southern Missouri's back country springs, punctuated by rivulets of trickling water that wander together willy-nilly to form rushing streams.

It abounds in great open spaces, where there is no place for sound to hide or find birth—like in western Missouri's flat prairies that stretch endlessly to a Kansas sunset.

It crackles in the aloneness, but not loneliness, of northern Missouri's fields under motionless cold.

It engulfs small Missouri towns on summer Sunday afternoons and it creeps into our cities in the dark of night.

But quiet need not, perhaps must not, be pursued overzealously or too far. It must be discovered, and its spirit-healing effects enjoyed wherever the mind is strong enough to shut out sound.

Quiet. More than a word, it is a rare and valuable commodity in today's decibel-rated world. But, like many of man's desires, it can elude him, like grasping a handful of morning mist, when he tries to hold it securely and permanently.

Duck's Ditty

Kenneth Grahame

All along the backwater,
   Through the rushes tall,
Ducks are a-dabbling,
   Up tails all!

Ducks' tails, drakes' tails,
   Yellow feet aquiver,
Yellow bills all out of sight,
   Busy in the river!

Slushy green undergrowth
   Where the roaches swim—
Here we keep our larder
   Cool and full and dim.

Everyone for what he likes!
   We like to be
Heads down, tails up,
   Dabbling free!

High in the blue above
   Swifts whirl and call—
We are down a-dabbling,
   Up tails all!

68

My Best Bouquet

Genevieve Sandifer Goodnow

"Mommy!" he called
One time, then two.
"Come and see what
I have for you!"

A handsome pride
In his voice rang out,
And quickly I answered
His vigorous shout.

With a smile that would make
The sunshine blush,
My three-year-old came
To my side with a rush.

"These flowers I found
In the yard for you.
There are some more—
I'll get them too!"

He hurried back
To the dandelion patch
For blossoms that never
A florist could match.

There are orchids and roses—
Choose what you may;
But dandelions make
My best bouquet.

FROM MY
G·A·R·D·E·N
JOURNAL

Deana Deck

I can't imagine spring without the rich, heady fragrance of lilacs drifting on the breeze. On the shores of Lake Superior where I first fell under their spell, they grow in great hedges along the streets and in wild clumps beside the kitchen doors of countless nineteenth-century homesteads. In early June the air for miles around is thickened with their luscious scent.

From the time of the Puritans onward, homesick settlers of this wild and mysterious new land brought along green scraps of their own childhood springtimes—the easily transported, easily planted lilac. By 1652 lilacs were growing throughout the colonies. In 1753 a recipient of a lilac as a gift from abroad complained that roots brought by earlier settlers had taken such a hold in this country that the lilac had become altogether too common a plant!

Every spring, descendants of these original plants burst into bloom throughout the Northeast, in the mountains of Appalachia, and across the Great Plains. They can be seen wherever the pioneers passed, except in the deserts and the Deep South, for the lilac must have water, and it must have winter.

When I set out to buy my first lilac, I knew nothing whatsoever about the plant except that I always wanted to live within sight of it. The nursery I visited had but two varieties—French and Persian. Unaware of the fact that there are thousands of lilac cultivars available, I selected the Persian, partly because it was lilac-colored (the French selection was white), and partly because of the name. I was seeking whatever lilac I could find that would fill my garden with that remembered intensity of fragrance, and it seemed reasonable to assume that a shrub with such an exotic aroma must have originated in the oriental splendor of a sultan's garden. I was wrong.

The most widely planted lilac varieties are descendants of *Syringa vulgaris*, which grows wild in the rocky, limestone soils of Rumania, Yugoslavia, and Moldavia. The only other native European lilac, the *S. josikea*, is found in the mountains of Transylvania, which includes portions of modern-day Hungary, Yugoslavia, and the old Austro-Hungarian Empire.

There are also a number of Asian species originating in China, India, Korea, and Japan. Many of these found their way into the gardens of European royalty around the mid-sixteenth century, but it was not until approximately one hundred years ago that hybridizers began to refine and perfect new varieties, and the popular hybrid known as the Persian lilac was created. In spite of a name which implies the sweet fragrance of the fabled oriental spices and oils of antiquity, the Persian can't hold a candle to *S. vulgaris*, a plant of uncommon virtue known, unfortunately, as the common lilac. This widely planted species remains the best flowering and most fragrant of them all.

If you live in a climate that offers normal rainfall and cold winters with plenty of snow, you live in lilac country, and your bushes will thrive in whatever sunny spot you plant them. Native to the mountainous, limestone-studded terrain of Eastern Europe and Asia, the lilac prefers a soil that is neutral or slightly alkaline. If your soil is acidic, you can compensate by adding a couple of handfuls of ground limestone to the root zone every third year.

Nothing, however, will compensate for soils that drain poorly. In soil with a high clay content a lilac will drown in a matter of weeks. If you are cursed with these conditions you will have to do some extensive soil amending or face life without the lilac. To me the choice is obvious.

In soils with a great deal of clay, plant lilacs as you would azaleas or rhododendrons—on top of the soil. First place a six-inch layer of sand and pea gravel at soil level, then continue to add layers of humus, composted manure, and garden soil until you have a gently sloping mound about two feet high. Set the lilacs on the mound, spread the roots over it gently, and add another eight inches of rich soil on top. Mulch with three to four inches of woodchips, sawdust, or straw. Leave a dish-like basin around the base of each shrub to catch water and avoid erosion of the mound.

In areas with mild drainage problems you can make do by filling the bottom third of the planting hole with a mixture of sand and pea gravel. Above this place a layer of sand and peat, then a loose mixture of the finest organic garden soil you can obtain. On these layers goes the plant, and it's a good idea to apply a mix of straw, gravel, and loose woodchips directly to the rootball. Lilacs send out masses of fibrous root hairs which require ample air spaces in the soil. In addition, water needs to have a clear pathway to the root zone and an equally clear path away from the roots. Let your plant drink as the water bubbles its way past on its way to some other destination.

One of the most tragic sights I have ever seen was a lilac being chain-sawed to the ground to make space for a kitchen addition to a 100-year-old farmhouse. The lilac is easily transplanted because all of the feeder roots tend to stay near the surface, none going deeper than the top foot and a half of soil. (The achoring roots go somewhat deeper, but the loss of a portion of these is not life-threatening.) In addition, the plant can be moved in the heat of summer, unlike most other shrubs. Provide good drainage, frequent and generous watering, and they will do just fine. It also helps if you top prune the shrub by about one third to ease the burden of the roots as they become established in the new location.

The best time to prune a lilac is right after it has finished blooming. It is important to select out all the branches that bore blossoms and cut them back as far as possible. Thus, the new shoots will receive the benefit of all the nutrients the plant takes up. Don't expect new blooms to appear on branches that have already produced. It won't happen.

All this growth of new wood and production of

buds demands ample nourishment, so provide your lilac with the richest organic compost you can find. Enrich the planting hole with it and add it to the base of the plant each spring. It also helps to scratch a handful of bonemeal into the soil, but don't dig deeply or you may damage the surface roots.

Lilacs are relatively pest-free. The most common problem you will encounter is powdery mildew. This can be prevented by using the same type of anti-fungal spray you apply to roses. Spray the lilac about every ten days, especially in humid weather. Another problem you may encounter is the lilac borer. The adults lay eggs inside the shrub's older wood where the larvae hatch out and burrow deeper into the branches. Sprays will control the borer in the adult stage, so they seldom kill a healthy lilac.

These may seem like too many deterrents for those who love lilacs, but when you think about it, a bushel of compost and a few gallons of water each year are a small price to pay for the incomparable scent of lilac drifting in from your own garden. It is a sensory experience that will grab hold of your heart and memory for all time.

Deana Deck reports on gardening techniques for The Tennessean *and has been a contributor to* Nashville Magazine. *She grows her lilacs in Nashville, Tennessee.*

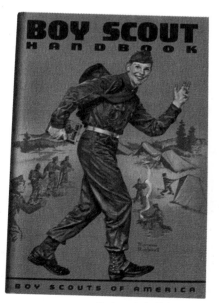

was a new picture on his easel. His pictures appeared everywhere. He painted portraits of famous people, of ordinary people; he illustrated books and calendars, playing cards and greeting cards, songsheets and billboards; he designed stamps for the United States Post Office and coins for the Franklin Mint; and he created advertisements for over 100 major corporations. Interest in Rockwell's advertising genius has inspired a book called *The Advertising World of Norman Rockwell,* published by Crown, Inc.

But Rockwell's main recognition came from his magazine covers and story illustrations. In addition to his well-known relationship with the *Saturday Evening Post,* for whom he did 323 covers between 1916 and 1963 when the magazine ceased publication, he worked for *Life, Look, Colliers, Country Gentleman, Literary Digest, Leslies, Judge, Farm Journal, Boy's Life,* and others. Vintage copies of all of his magazine work are much sought after by collectors; but to acquire every one of the *Saturday Evening Post* covers is a collector's dream. Although the magazine sold for only a nickle or a dime, a complete collection of original covers in good condition

A collection built around the work of Norman Rockwell is a joy to behold. Norman Rockwell's name is synonymous with nostalgia, holidays, happy times, family fun, patriotism, and all things good. What adult doesn't remember reading the *Saturday Evening Post* when Norman Rockwell was creating his memorable covers for them? What doctor's office doesn't display a picture of a little girl letting the doctor examine her doll, or of a little boy with his pants down, about to get a shot? What school doesn't have pictures of Rockwell's "Four Freedoms" on its walls? What Boy Scout doesn't remember the Norman Rockwell cover on his official handbook?

In fact, Norman Rockwell created nearly five thousand pictures over a span of six decades. He painted and sketched relentlessly from 1914, when he submitted his first drawings for the Boy Scout manual, to his death in 1978, at which time there

Photography by Donald Stoltz

is worth many thousands of dollars today.

For the avid collector, an original Norman Rockwell oil painting is a prized possession. Although most of his paintings are now in museums and galleries, many originals are in the homes of private individuals, and a few are still available for sale from respected art dealers such as Judy Goffman of New York City. However, these paintings can range from $20,000 for a story illustration to well over $100,000 for an original oil painting of a *Saturday Evening Post* cover.

But a Rockwell collection needn't be focused on originals. His unique and expressive images of the parades, the parties, the picnics, the war years and peaceful times, the presidents and movie stars, the babies and grandparents have all spawned reproductions galore. Beautiful porcelain figurines inspired by Rockwell illustrations are reproduced with painstaking accuracy. These affordable collectibles are available in various sizes and shapes. Equally handsome are several series of plates, bowls, mugs, trays, and tankards adorned with Norman Rockwell classics. Of course, these are not Rockwell "originals"—except for a series created by the Franklin Mint, "The Joys of Childhood." Most porcelain products are not authorized or designed by the late artist, but they capture the spirit of his paintings and are treasured by collectors.

There are many reasons why people collect things, but Norman Rockwell memorabilia is collected for a special reason above and beyond the

value, beauty, rarity, nostalgia, and good investment to be had. These pieces are the work of a true and distinctly American genius, the likes of which we may never see again.   Dr. Donald Stoltz

Dr. Donald Stoltz is the President of the Norman Rockwell Museum in Philadelphia, Pennsylvania.

BITS &

There is nothing grander, more beautiful, more inspiring than the love of a good mother. She caresses the infant at her knee; she nourishes it until it has strength to stand and prattle at her side; she watches over and protects the child from harm while it remains under her care; and when it goes out in the world, her love follows.

Samual Smiles

Don't object that your duties are so insignificant. They are to be reckoned of infinite significance, and alone important to you. Were it but the perfect regulation of your apartment, the sorting away of your clothes and trinkets, the arranging of your papers; whatever thy hand findeth to do, do it with all thy might, and all thy worth and constancy.

Thomas Carlyle

Heaven lies about us in our infancy.

William Wordsworth

Ten thousand tedious trifles attended to; ten thousand orders given and disappointments borne, go to the making up of a triumph.

* * *

All common things, each day's events,
    That with the hour begin and end,
Our pleasures and our discontents,
    Are rounds by which we may ascend.

Henry Wadsworth Longfellow

It is true that the sacrifices that women make for the world will be little known by it. Men govern and earn the glory; and the thousand watchful nights and sacrifices by which a mother purchases a hero or a poet for the state are forgotten—not one counted, for the mothers themselves do not count them; and so, one century after another, do mothers, unnamed and unthanked, send forth the arrows, the suns, the storm-birds, and the nightingales of time.

Jean Paul Richter

PIECES

Childhood has no forebodings; but then, it is soothed by no memories of outlived sorrow.

George Eliot

By desiring what is perfectly good, even when we do not quite know what it is and cannot do what we would, we are part of the divine power against evil in the skirts of light and making the struggle with darkness narrower.

George Eliot

A partnership with God is motherhood;
What strength, what purity, what self-control,
What love, what wisdom should belong to her
Who helps God fashion an immortal soul.

Anonymous

Those love truth best who to themselves are true,
And what they dare to dream of, dare to do.

* * *

Life is too short for us to waste its moments in deploring bad luck; we must go after success, since it will not come to us, and we have no time to spare.

* * *

Good luck is the willing handmaid of upright, energetic character and conscientious observance of duty.

James Russell Lowell

As the vexations men receive from their children hasten the approach of age and double the force of years, so the comforts they reap from them are balm to all their sorrows and disappoint the injuries of time. Parents repeat their lives in their offspring; and their esteem for them is so great that they feel their sufferings and taste their enjoyments as much as if they were their own.

Ray Palmer

Children do not know how their parents love them, and they never will till the grave closes over those parents, or till they have children of their own.

P. Cooke

Photo Overleaf
AZALEAS
CALLAWAY GARDENS, GEORGIA
Dietrich Photography

Love Companions Me

Mary Pollard Tynes

Now I walk with gladness
  If skies be blue or gray,
And find a joy in sun or rain
  To comfort me each day.

I greet the pink of dawning
  With deeper, keener zest,
And through each passing hour
  Toil, smile, and do my best.

And as the years move slowly
  They bring life's ecstasy
Beneath a sky of blue or gray,
  For love companions me!

Give Thanks
for These

Johanna Ter Wee

For scented lilacs in the spring
When new life wakens everything,
For geese in migratory flight,
And stars that warm a deep blue night;

For rocks and boulders etched by time,
For panoramic views sublime;
Mountains, lakes, and tumbling streams,
Beauty beyond our fondest dreams;

For firesides and homey things,
And joy that soars on golden wings.

Readers' Forum

As an almost-octogenarian, I have taken Ideals for many, many years. I never cease to marvel at the beautiful photography, the high-quality art work, articles, and poetry. I would not want to do without my "red-letter days"—the days my Ideals arrive.

Mrs. Marion Lawrence
Monetville, Ontario

I live in a retirement residence and a few of us here are a bit uncertain about the authorship of the "First Letter Home" published in your Thanksgiving issue. Some of us have doubts about its authenticity while others think it probably was a glorified copy of an honest letter. In either situation, wouldn't it require some kind of acknowledgement as to the original author?

Mrs. M. G. Austin
Vernon, Vermont

The author responds: Elizabeth Hopkins really existed. She made the crossing on the Mayflower with her husband, and her son, Oceanus, was born on shipboard. Everything described in my piece is truthful and accurate. I hoped that readers would get a real sense of how difficult the crossing was for the Pilgrims, and of what it felt like to be a young woman at that time in history. I was inspired to speak in Elizabeth's voice by the exhibit in Plymouth, Massachusetts, of an exact replica of the Mayflower, where people in period costumes represent each person who actually crossed the ocean and are well-versed in what their character would know about the trip from England. I interviewed several of the women and also researched journals and other documents from the period. I have no way of knowing whether a letter like this was written by Elizabeth, but it *could* have been written.

Pamela Kennedy
Honolulu, Hawaii

Thank you so much for the years of pleasure your lovely magazine has brought me. As a former teacher of English, I have a great love for literature. Your magazine has faithfully presented lovely poems and prose with beautiful pictures to accompany them. I have collected years of Ideals dating back to the early issues. I keep them proudly on display in my front sitting room so that special company can see them. My issues of thirty years ago are just as beautiful as those of three years ago. Please continue to present this gorgeous collection.

Minnie M. Brunson
Tupelo, Mississippi

I just had to write to tell you how much I enjoy the poems and short stories in Ideals. There are many that express exactly how I feel. Sometimes I am overwhelmed by the beauty and emotions of the words, and I can't help the tears in my eyes. . . . Please continue to publish those wonderful poems and stories—they certainly put "sunshine" in my day!

Geraldine Haniff
Sarnia, Ontario
Canada

* * *

CRAFTWORKS

Readers are invited to submit original craft ideas for possible development and publication in future *Ideals* issues. Please send query letter with idea (and photograph, if available) to "Craftworks," Ideals Publishing Corporation, P.O. Box 140300, Nashville, Tennessee 37214-0300. Do not send samples; they cannot be returned.

Upon acceptance, writers must supply design, text instructions, and sample product. Payment will vary accordingly and will be upon publication.

ideals
Celebrating Life's Most Treasured Moments

Special Offer to *Ideals* Subscribers

Occasionally, we run across a book that is so beautiful and so attuned to the values of *Ideals* that we simply must offer it to our subscribers. Better Homes and Gardens *American Patchwork & Quilting* is just such a book. This treasury of quilting is specially designed to inspire and instruct both beginners and experts with its beautiful color photographs and over 200 diagrams and patterns for your convenience. This volume also contains helpful hints on piecing, quilting, and displaying quilts and other household and gift items, along with an essential glossary of terms. The easy-to-follow instructions will guide you as you discover your talents for creating through patchwork and quilting.

To order your copy of *American Patchwork & Quilting,* just tear off the card at the right, fill in your name and address, and mail for your trial examination of this lovely publication.

- 320 oversize pages
- over 243 full-color photographs
- 65 step-by-step how-to photos illustrating techniques of piecing, appliqué, and quilting
- 256 patterns and diagrams
- 193 projects
- 217 patchwork designs

Now, you can learn how to create heirloom-quality patchwork masterpieces you'll treasure for years to come.

Plus a FREE GIFT
just for reviewing AMERICAN
PATCHWORK & QUILTING
with no obligation to buy

NO POSTAGE
NECESSARY
IF MAILED
IN THE
UNITED STATES

BUSINESS REPLY MAIL
FIRST CLASS MAIL   PERMIT NO. 5761   NASHVILLE, TN

POSTAGE WILL BE PAID BY ADDRESSEE

IDEALS PUBLISHING CORPORATION
Nelson Place at Elm Hill Pike
P.O. Box 148000
Nashville, TN 37214-9988